LOST PUBS

OF HULL

Paul Gibson and GrahamWilkinson

Kingston **Press**

British Library Cataloguing in Publication Data.
A catalogue record for this book is available from the British Library.

First published 1999

© 1999 Paul Gibson and Graham Wilkinson
All photographs © respective owners as indicated

Published by Kingston Press

ISBN 1 902039 03 3

Kingston Press is the publishing imprint of Kingston upon Hull City Libraries,
Central Library, Albion Street, Kingston upon Hull, England HU1 3TF

Printed by Kingston upon Hull City Council Printing Services,
1-5 Witham, Kingston upon Hull, England HU9 1DA

Front cover: The Oriental Hotel, Hedon Road, page 93

ACKNOWLEDGEMENTS

The authors wish to thank Christopher Ketchell, a very nice man to whom the city of Hull owes a large debt, Gail Thornton, for tea, cake, computing facilities and patience, Geoff Oxley, Elspeth Rippon and the team at Hull City Archives, David Smith and his ever-helpful staff at Hull Local Studies Library, Clare Parsons and Jayne Tyler at Wilberforce House Museum, Jack, Annie, Gertie and Rita for occupational therapy.

We are grateful to the following who have given permission to use the photographs as indicated:

Bob Burton (photographs from the 'Hull Brewery collection'): 1, 5, 9, 12, 13, 16, 19, 23, 24, 25, 26, 27, 29, 30, 31, 32, 34, 35, 37, 38, 39, 41, 43, 44, 46, 48, 51, 52, 54, 55, 56, 59, 61, 62, 65, 68, 69, 70, 71, 72, 76, 77, 78, 79, 80, 81, 82, 85, 86, 88, 89, 90, 91, 92, 95, 96, 98, 99, 101, 102, 104, 105.

Kingston upon Hull City Council, Archives/City Records Office: 6(TPP/64/32),7, 14, 15, 20, 21(TSP739/9), 28(TSP/236), 42, 49, 50(TPP/5/93).

Kingston upon Hull City Council, Museums & Libraries: 3, 4, 8(680), 10, 11(436-1981-2), 17, 22, 53(622-1981-4), 60, 63, 66(861), 67(884), 84(605-1981-6), 100(1365), 103(1408).

John Wyles collection: 18, 33, 36, 47, 58, 64, 75, 94.

Paul Gibson collection: 40, 73, 83, 87, 97.

Memory Lane Photographic Gallery: 2, 45, 57 (All available as prints from their gallery on the Hessle Road).

Frank Farnsworth collection: 93.

Mr. Neilsen collection: 74.

John Wm. Gibson at the bar of the County Hotel, Charles Street.

This book is dedicated to

Paul's parents Jack and Annie Gibson and John William Gibson, his grandfather, who "liked a pint".

and

Graham's parents Harry and Mary Wilkinson who both loved their Mild and Stout

CONTENTS

Introduction

INTRODUCTION

Several "local history/interest" books are published each year in Hull and thus far few have touched on an aspect of Hull's social history that has run as a thread through the lives of many local people - its pubs.

This book is intended simply as an illustration of a sample of those pubs, which for many reasons are no longer with us. Hopefully it will serve as a reminder of the variety of types and styles of pub, which featured as part of the Hull landscape, as well as a nostalgic step back in time. It is not intended as an academic study of the pub, more a pictorial reference of what were, for the large part, fondly remembered buildings.

Due to changes in fashion and the demands of today's society, many surviving 'old' pubs have been repeatedly refurbished and in many cases ill-conceived alterations have often led to the loss of many unique and irreplaceable features. Recently a trend towards preservation by the owners has begun another, more positive, change in fashion.

Sadly the character of most newly-built pubs has little to compare with those lost. This is due, in the most part, to modern demands and the sheer scale of the new buildings, rather than any design faults. Safety requirements and ease of management now place specific demands on structural design that leave little scope for authentic reproduction and it would be unfair to expect any architect to recapture a moment in time.

Pubs have featured in the workaday routine of the Hull populace for centuries and in the last two or three decades have become accepted as a place for social gatherings and relaxation by a much wider spectrum of people, so much so that it is estimated that over two million of us drink in them every day. It would seem the traditional 'English pub' is not as yet an endangered species.

The pub we know today has evolved from an often confusing variety of establishments, which became common during the 18th and 19th centuries, particularly the alehouse and the tavern. Indeed the now familiar term 'pub' (an abbreviation of 'public house') is likely to have been a corruption of the term 'public alehouse'. Therefore, for the purposes of this book, the term 'pub' has been used to describe the majority of the premises illustrated. However, the following list is a brief summary of some of the other terms that have been used historically. As there were many others in use at different periods, these simplified descriptions are merely intended as illustrative outlines.

Alehouse: An ancient term used to describe a house licensed to sell beer, wine and spirits for consumption on and off the premises, which may also have provided accommodation.

Beer-house: A house licensed to sell only beer and cider, following the so-called Beer-House Act of 1830.

Dram shop: Usually smaller premises, which purported to sell only spirits.

Hotel: An often misused term in use from the late 18th century, which implied an inn of higher quality, that also provided food and lodgings.

Inn: A place that provided food and lodgings predominantly for travellers on horseback or in horse-drawn transport.

Tap: A smaller pub attached to an inn, usually for the working classes and often with its own separate licence.

Tavern: A house that sold beer, wine and spirits, which was similar to an alehouse and generally accommodated those on foot.

There have also been many terms used to describe the person who controlled these establishments, who most people would have referred to as the 'landlord'. In most cases in this book, the more accurate term licensee, licensed victualler or victualler has been used – a person providing food and/or drink on licensed premises.

Historically Hull had what might be described as a love-hate relationship with its pubs. Alehouses were licensed from the 16th century in one form or another and as early as 1560 the 'bench' (an early version of the City Council) was convinced that public morals would be much improved if ale was weaker and less was drunk. The members of the bench were able to exert strict control over the alehouses in the town, which at that time was still confined within the town walls.

In 1574 there were only ten inns and twenty-nine alehouses within the town and despite the feelings of the bench, numbers continued to rise. By 1630 when Hull's population was still less than 6,000, there were forty-two alehouses in the town and by the end of the century the number had almost doubled. The members of the bench faced an uphill struggle.

Whilst the upper classes, with their comfortable homes, had their own clubs and entertainment, the lower classes had little in comparison. Their sport was usually found at the alehouses in the form of bear-baiting, dog-fighting, cock-fighting and various forms of gambling, although the latter was popular with both classes. The local alehouse or tavern provided welcome respite from the squalor of the working man's own home. The dry warmth, light and companionship of an alehouse was preferable to home for the average working man and often the rest of his family. Gradually a society grew which revolved very much around the drinking houses. Those profiting from the alehouses were quick to realise that the comfort and warmth they offered was directly proportional to the length of time spent drinking by the public. Many alehouses and taverns had rear doors that opened directly into the court housing of the poor, enticing them from their very homes. An unhealthy alliance was sometimes formed between employers and the alehouses with men being paid their wages in the bars and often on a Saturday. At this time beer was 1s per gallon and a poor man's wage was around 15s a week. Temptation was everywhere.

From 1729 the Brewster Sessions began regulating the number of licensed premises but even so the numbers rose dramatically from 103 in 1740 to 187 in 1794. As the population increased towards the end of the century, new development spread north and west beyond the town walls. This development and the massive increase in Hull's population (which had grown to over 22,000 by 1801) saw an even sharper increase in the number of licensed premises.

The problems associated with drink, particularly chronic illness and violent crime, were causing great concern throughout England, particularly due to the excessive consumption of gin and other spirits. The previously haphazard legislation was tightened by the Alehouse Act of 1828 and more importantly the so-called Beer-house Act of 1830. This sought to draw the public away from spirits and restrict the hours during which alcohol could be consumed. Sadly, but not unpredictably, the Act misfired. Whilst attempting to control the drinking hours, it enabled almost anyone to sell beer (now free from tax) on payment of the two guinea licence fee. Hence the number of licensed and approved premises soared, so much so that in 1853 there were over 500 in Hull alone.

Hull was alleged to have one beer-house for every twenty dwelling houses, more than any other town of its size. Most of these were badly managed and disorderly. These so-called "Tom and Jerry" or "Swankey" houses opened everywhere, which led Sydney Smith to write: *The new Beer Bill begun its operations. Everybody is drunk. The sovereign people are in a beastly state*.

Despite an amendment to the Act in1834, which resulted in a distinction between 'on' and 'off' licences, it was not until 1840 that some form of control was regained in the third Beer-house Act. This Act specified that a new licence could not be issued unless the applicant was the resident holder and occupier of the premises concerned. This served to limit the ever-increasing numbers, which were impossible to police. By 1869, there were 53,000 beer-houses in England and the numbers were increasing at a rate of 2,000 per year.

Further control came with the Licensing Acts of 1865 and 1872, both influenced heavily by the growing tide of drink reformers. The aim of both Acts was to limit opening hours and this was bitterly resented by the public. The resentment was so deeply felt that the Act of 1872 led to rioting in the streets of Hull and other towns throughout the country. Following the Act of 1872, pubs opened at five in the morning and closed at midnight, except on Saturdays when they closed at eleven and did not open again until noon on Sunday. Prior to this there had been virtually no restrictions at all.

The 1872 Act also *"disallowed the sale of spirits for the consumption on the premises to those apparently under the age of 16"*. It had not been unusual for children of twelve to fourteen to spend much of their time in beer-houses, many of which had rooms especially for their younger drinkers, often with steps to the bar counter.

The effect of the various Acts and the shadow of the temperance movement led to a steady decline in the number of new licences as the century wore on. In 1905 a new Act, 'The Balfour Closure & Compensation Act' had a further effect in the trade of 'old for new' pubs. If a new pub was to open in the growing suburbs, this meant that one, or often two, would be forced to close elsewhere, usually in the overcrowded Old Town. Hull began to lose its pubs.

The majority of the buildings in this collection of photographs date from the 19th century when the pub as we know it began to evolve. Earlier establishments had developed from vernacular buildings with the exception of the coaching inns and during the first years of the 19th century there would have been little to distinguish some licensed premises from dwelling houses, apart from an occasional sign over the door. Internally the emphasis would have been on seating with drink being served from a separate room or cellar. The use of a counter became common in later years and was often no more than planks of wood or a door placed over up-turned barrels.

Shop fronts, with displays to entice the drinker and large lamps over the door to guide them in, began a trend for exterior decoration. This swiftly developed, as competition between the premises grew. Internally, the continued licensing restrictions caused pubs to create separate rooms for more effective management by the increased numbers of staff. A variety of rooms appeared; smoke rooms, snugs, public and private bars, tap rooms and even concert rooms - the forerunners of the Music Hall. The division between the working class and the 'new' lower middle class was further widened, as houses began to divide their interiors into separate and smaller rooms.

As the larger breweries began their interest in acquiring the smaller pubs, many began to employ their own architects and designers. Prior to this quality architects, fearing the wrath of the temperance societies, rarely dared to design a pub. The task of drawing up the plans for conversions and even purpose-built premises often fell to the builder himself. This led to an enormous variation in quality and by the turn of the century, the subsequent variation in appearance was enormous - from the simple beer-house front to the decadence of the so-called 'Gin Palaces'. Often elements of the two combined to create interesting one-offs and endless choice for the public.

Changes in fashion, slum clearance programmes and the devastation of World War 2 have all played a part in the loss of Hull's pub heritage in the 20th century. Few, if any, original beer-houses survive and many of the later Victorian and Edwardian conversions that do bear little resemblance to their former selves. An incredible number of architectural gems are now lost forever. Some live on in the memories of those who were lucky enough to have caught a glimpse before they fell. This book contains a small selection of photographs from my own and other collections that will hopefully jog memories, begin debate and no doubt promote healthy argument.

Paul Gibson
November 1999

SECTION 1: THE OLD TOWN

THE OLD TOWN: LOCATION MAP

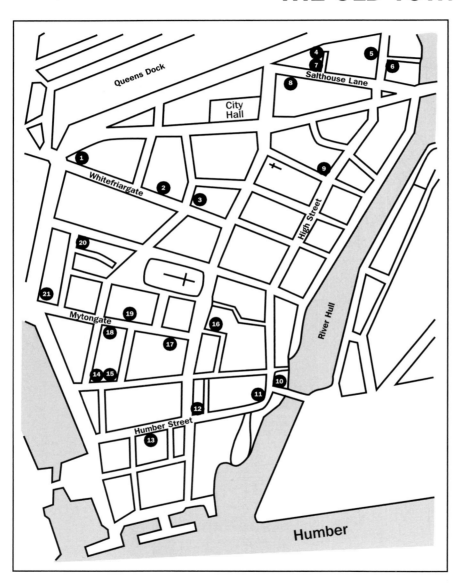

1. MONUMENT TAVERN, WHITEFRIARGATE
2. GEORGE HOTEL, WHITEFRIARGATE
3. CROWN & CUSHION INN, LAND OF GREEN GINGER
4. FULL SHIP INN, NORTH WALLS
5. HIGHLAND LADDIE, HIGH STREET
6. TIGRESS INN, HIGH STREET
7. SHIP & PLOUGH INN, SALTHOUSE LANE
8. PINEAPPLE INN, SALTHOUSE LANE
9. EDINBURGH PACKET INN, HIGH STREET
10. DOG & DUCK INN, HIGH STREET
11. GEORGE & DRAGON INN, HIGH STREET
12. ALEXANDRA HOTEL, HUMBER STREET
13. SHAKESPEARE HOTEL, HUMBER STREET
14. HAMBURG TAVERN, BLANKET ROW
15. NAVIGATION INN, BLANKET ROW
16. MARROWBONE & CLEAVER INN, FETTER LANE
17. TIVOLI HOTEL, MYTONGATE
18. IMPERIAL MEASURE INN, MYTONGATE
19. RAMPANT HORSE INN, MYTONGATE
20. SOCIETY TAVERN, DAGGER LANE
21. PUNCH INN, PRINCES DOCK SIDE

1. MONUMENT TAVERN, WHITEFRIARGATE

The Monument Tavern stood on the north side of Whitefriargate, at No.37. Evidence exists to suggest that an alehouse or tavern of some description had stood on this site since the early 18th century.

The building shown in this photograph of circa 1925 was a rebuilt structure of the early 19th century and was listed in the trade directories from the 1820s. At this time it was known as the Old Andrew Marvel, changing its name to the York Tavern then the Wilberforce Wine Vaults, before settling on the name Monument Tavern around 1851. The latter names were both references to the monument erected in honour of the famous Hull MP and abolitionist William Wilberforce. Note the model of the monument between the first floor windows.

The pub remained open into the 1960s and is now the site of a CD and music store.

2. GEORGE HOTEL, WHITEFRIARGATE

The building we know today as the George pub in the Land of Green Ginger is in fact the remains of the George Hotel Tap, which stood to the rear of the much larger and grander George Hotel at No.66 Whitefriargate.

The George Hotel was the last of a long line of inns and taverns that had stood on the site since the 17th century. The owners at the turn of the 19th century, the Wooley family, rebuilt the hotel and tap. British Home Stores altered the main structure and frontage of the hotel in Whitefriargate after they purchased the site in 1932.

The George Hotel Tap, in the Land of Green Ginger, is all that remains of the 1800s rebuild. In 1936 the tap was taken over by Moors' & Robson's who bought the lease for £11,000 from J. Motion & Sons Ltd., the last owners of the George Hotel.

3. CROWN & CUSHION INN, LAND OF GREEN GINGER

The history of the Crown & Cushion is one of two separate public houses. The Crown was built circa 1800 and was entered from a passage at the side of No.17 Silver Street. Around 1823 it was renamed the Crown & Cushion.

By 1830 it had amalgamated with the White Lion at No.3 Land of Green Ginger, which backed onto the Crown & Cushion. The two continued until 1876 when the Crown & Cushion Silver Street was demolished for the construction of the London and Yorkshire Bank (later the National and Provincial Union Bank and currently the Nat West buildings). At this point the former White Lion took the name of the Crown & Cushion.

On 3rd September 1927 the pub closed when it was demolished for an extension to the bank building. The picture shows the shop front, and passage entrance from the Land of Green Ginger.

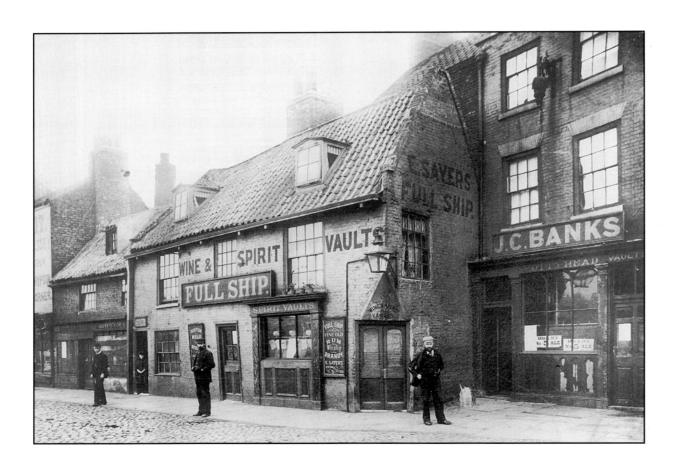

4. FULL SHIP INN, NORTH WALLS

The Full Ship is probably one of the oldest building in this collection. The address 'North Walls' indicates that it was situated on the site of the northern town walls, which were demolished prior to the construction of Queens Dock (now Queens Gardens) during the 1770s. This gives an earliest possible date for the group of buildings shown in this photograph of circa 1890.

Initially named the White Swan, it soon took on a nautical name to suit its situation overlooking the dockside. To the right can be seen another inn, the Scott's Head. Both were demolished in the late 19th century to be replaced by the larger Royal Sovereign public house.

The location would now be to the south of the Hull College Queens Gardens site.

5. HIGHLAND LADDIE, HIGH STREET

It is likely that an inn had stood on this site for some years prior to its earliest records in the 19th century trade directories. Situated at No.197 High Street, it was listed from 1803 when it was known as the Golden Fleece, victualler John Hewson. From 1826 it became known as simply The Fleece and by 1907 it had become the Highland Laddie.

The passage to the right of the door of the pub led to the yard of the North End Brewery, which had had connections with the Golden Fleece at the end of the 18th century.

Following a general decline in the area the pub closed at 3pm on the 7th December 1961 and the new Highland Laddie, Newbridge Road, opened at 6pm the same day. The site is now rebuilt and it is hard to imagine that a pub of this size ever stood on the spot.

6. TIGRESS INN, HIGH STREET

Diagonally opposite the Highland Laddie, at the south-west corner of Blaydes Staithe was the Tigress Inn, No.7 High Street. Known from the turn of the 19th century as the Blue Ball it later became the Ball, the Full Measure, the Corn Exchange Tavern and the New Exchange Tavern before becoming the Tigress Inn around 1867.

Although it appeared from the outside to be a small one-roomed inn, the Tigress also occupied property to the rear of No.8 High Street. The entry to the right of the pub led via a passage to a small yard at the rear of the buildings. The Tigress was a very popular Moors' & Robson's pub tucked away in what became known as 'Little High Street' but was nonetheless closed in 1971 and subsequently demolished.

7. SHIP & PLOUGH INN, SALTHOUSE LANE

This pub was first recorded in the trade directories as the Sir John Moore around 1813. Later known as the Plough & Sail, it became the Ship & Plough in the 1830s.

The picture gives its own visual clues to the age and history of the buildings, which were on the north side of Salthouse Lane. The 'ghosts' of the demolished buildings, recorded by the outline of their roofs, suggest that the property had been built many years before.

The fine glazed front was fitted in 1912 at a cost of £50, but only 10 years later the pub was closed. The building survived for many years and was used by a variety of small businesses before being demolished in the 1960s.

8. PINEAPPLE INN, SALTHOUSE LANE

The Pineapple Inn stood on the south side of Salthouse Lane, at its former junction with Lowgate. Although an ancient site, the inn was only recorded in the trade directories from 1803, when it was known as the Old Queens Head.

After changing its name to the Queen Caroline and then to the Whitby Tavern, it became the Pineapple around 1870, which it remained until its closure in 1916. At that time it was owned by Hewitt Brothers of Grimsby who claimed £1,330 compensation but were paid only £700.

The site is now within the car park on the east side of Lowgate, near the Gulidhall.

9. EDINBURGH PACKET INN, HIGH STREET

The Edinburgh Packet was situated at No. 163 High Street on the north corner of Chapel Lane and held a full alehouse licence. The earliest records of the pub are from the first years of the 19th century but it is very likely that the property was of a much earlier period.

The windows of the neighbouring property in Chapel Lane suggest a date of before 1705, when an ordinance required that windows be set back from the facing surface of walls. Although the windows of the Edinburgh Packet facing Chapel Lane are of a later design, the brickwork on the High Street frontage appears to be contemporary with that of its neighbour.

The pub closed in 1929 following a purge on licensed premises in the Old Town and £3,000 was paid to the Hull Brewery Co. in compensation for their loss of business.

10. DOG & DUCK INN, HIGH STREET

The Dog & Duck was latterly a Worthington's pub with a full alehouse licence. Many of the old inns and taverns of the Old Town held licences dating back hundreds of years. Although only recorded in the trade directories from 1803 it had probably been an inn for many years prior.

Situated on the east side of High Street just south of the junction with Blackfriargate, it had not always stood on a corner. The property to its right was taken down in 1864 to provide access for the South Bridge, which was constructed in 1865.

The name 'Dog & Duck' came from the 18th century 'sport' in which a duck's wings were tied before being thrown into the nearest pond or stream, at which point dogs were set upon it. The sport was banned but the name remained until the closure of the pub in 1908.

11. GEORGE & DRAGON INN, HIGH STREET

Local postcard publishers Parrish & Berry of Waltham Street, Hull took this picture of the George & Dragon in 1903. It shows quite clearly that the building was 'jettied' suggesting it was a timber framed property of at least the 15th century, although the building was only recorded as an inn from the end of the 18th century.

A small brewery operated from the rear of the George & Dragon in the 1830s and 1840s, a common feature of many public houses in the town.

The painted advertisement next to the door reads: "The noted house for lager beer, on draught and in bottles". The large gas lamp shown to the right of the photograph hung from the Dog & Duck, which stood almost opposite (see page 10).

The pub closed circa 1908 and was demolished in the early 1920s.

12. ALEXANDRA HOTEL, HUMBER STREET

Humber Street was so called because it had at one time been the most southern part of the town following the line of the town walls, beyond which was the River Humber.

Originally known, as the Humber Tavern the pub was a rebuild of a much older building that had stood on the site for many years. The tavern changed name during the 1860s, possibly in recognition of the marriage of Princess Alexandra of Denmark to Albert Edward, Prince of Wales, in 1863.

The Alexandra was also used as a booking agency for the various steam packets that used the port, as were many of the pubs in the Old Town. The Alexandra Hotel closed on 12th February 1927 and the site is now a car park east of the junction with Queen Street.

The premises of the well known marine photographer and postcard publisher M.Barnard can be seen to the left of this photograph taken circa 1925.

13. SHAKESPEARE HOTEL, HUMBER STREET

The Shakespeare Hotel was situated on the south side of Humber Street, in the heart of what is now Hull's fruit market area. Following the development of this section of Humber Street, during the first years of the 19th century, the area thrived. A new theatre, the Theatre Royal was opened in Humber Street in 1810 and was no doubt the inspiration for the name of this pub, the Shakespeare Tavern, which opened in the same year.

In stark contrast the Humber Street Wesley Chapel was built to the west in 1832 and the tavern, now sandwiched between these two grand buildings, elevated its title to that of hotel during the 1840s. In a later refurbishment, probably in the late 1890s six carved heads of Shakespeare were added to the rather plain frontage, all of which can be seen in this photograph of circa 1925.

The Shakespeare closed following heavy bomb damage sustained in an air raid on the 9th May 1941.

14. HAMBURG TAVERN, BLANKET ROW

Situated on the north side of Blanket Row at No.25 was the Hamburg Tavern. It was first mentioned in the trade directories circa 1813 as the Town & Trade of Hull, but by 1826 had become the Billy Boy.

Further changes of name followed during the 1830s, the Lamb, the Tam O' Shanter and from 1838 the Hamburg Tavern, which it remained until its closure circa 1908.

The Police had objected to the renewal of its licence in 1907 when £1,220 was paid in compensation when the objection was upheld. The building survived for many years, having being taken over by the neighbouring butcher's business almost immediately after closure.

This photograph of 1938 shows the Hamburg Tavern occupied by John Fisher, wholesale butcher, whose slaughterhouse can be seen to the left at the corner of Sewer Lane.

15. NAVIGATION INN, BLANKET ROW

Humber Dock, the second of Hull's docks was opened on the 30th June 1809 and gave rise to several new pub names. An alehouse, the aptly named 'New Dock Opening', was recorded at No.29 Blanket Row in 1810.

By 1834 the name had changed to the Leeds Tavern and by 1874 to the Navigation Inn. As the photograph shows, the property was very small. Originally occupying only the left-hand half of the property shown, it took over the shop next door in the early 1890s. The centre door with etched glass window led to a small court which had been known as Bean's Square, Haynes' Court and following the expansion of the inn, Navigation Court.

The humble buildings survived both World Wars and closed in the early 1970s.

16. MARROWBONE & CLEAVER INN, FETTER LANE

The aptly named Marrowbone & Cleaver had stood at the side of the old meat and fish market 'Shambles' in Fetter Lane for decades prior to its first record in the trade directories in the 1820s.

Fetter Lane as the title implied (fetters were a type of shackle for the feet) had also held a House of Correction and criminals may have been held in fetters outside the building.

The pub name was probably second choice as there was already a Butchers Arms within the Shambles buildings in Blackfriargate Alley. It was however, a common name; there is a Marrowbone and Cleaver in London today and curiously it also has the address Fetter Lane.

The pub survived long after the covered market had transferred to its present site, not closing until the 4th March 1957. The site of Fetter Lane is now a car park opposite the statue of King William III in the Market Place soon, to house Hull's new Courthouse buildings.

17. TIVOLI HOTEL, MYTONGATE

The Bull & Sun Hotel had stood at No.1 Mytongate since the 17th century when it was mentioned in deeds as the Seven Stars. It was later one of 14 pubs shown in Mytongate on the first Ordnance Survey plan of Hull issued in 1853.

Changing its name to the Black Bull (a name derived from the sport of bull baiting which was popular at many inns) and from the 1790s to the Bull & Sun, the inn had been one of Hull's principal coaching houses and many of the local carriers used it as a pick up point for the transportation of passengers and goods all over the district.

In 1895 it became the Tivoli Hotel and in 1899 it was tied to Worthington's Brewery, having previously sold Allsopp's Ales.

It survived into the 1960s finally closing in 1967 when the licence was given up for the Silver Cod pub on Anlaby Road.

18. IMPERIAL MEASURE INN, MYTONGATE

If the number of inns and taverns that served a street were a gauge of its importance, then Mytongate having around 23 at one time or another was second only to High Street.

On the south side of Mytongate, between Sewer Lane and Finkle Street, was the pub known as the Imperial Measure. It appeared in the directories around 1820 known as the Golden Cup but by 1826 had changed its name to the Full Measure under the new victualler, wine and spirit merchant John Christie late of the Societies Tavern, Dagger Lane. In the years following it became known as the Imperial Measure but was more commonly known by the name of 'Christie's'.

The Christie family held the premises with a full alehouse licence for approximately 60 years until circa 1887.

The pub continued trading as the Imperial Measure Inn into the 20th century, finally closing on the 1st July 1929 following a purge on licensed premises in the Old Town.

19. RAMPANT HORSE INN, MYTONGATE

This pub was originally known as the Full Measure, one of the most common names for a public house. By 1826 it had become the Rampant Horse under a new victualler Joseph Dinsdale. The name Rampant Horse could possibly have been taken from the coat of arms of a previous owner of the property.

The large opening to the left of the bar led to Dinsdales' Entry, named after the Dinsdale family who ran the pub for more than thirty years. Within the entry were livery stables belonging to the pub.

The Rampant Horse closed in 1966 but the building survived as the last pub building on Mytongate until 1989 when the site was redeveloped for the Grammar School Yard housing complex.

20. SOCIETY TAVERN, DAGGER LANE

The Society Tavern or Hotel stood on Dagger Lane at the corner of Prince Street. Although a very old inn, it was only recorded in the trade directories from 1803.

The Society retained its name throughout its life until October 1961 when it closed following a general decline of trade in the area. The licence was removed to the new Crows Nest on Douglas Road.

During the 1950s the Society had been known as 'Freddie Nunn's' (the name of a popular licensee), and after closure it became the Crackovianka until it was drastically restructured in 1984 to form the Lanes shopping arcade. This picture shows it at the height of its popularity in the 1930's.

21. PUNCH INN, PRINCES DOCK SIDE

This 1940s photograph of the corner of Princes Dock Side or Street shows that the old street sign with its former name 'Junction Dock Street' had remained long after the street changed its name circa 1861.

The building shown adjoining the barbers is No.1 Princes Dock Street formerly the Punch Inn, which had first opened in the late 1860s. It had previously been the premises of furniture broker John Dobson and his descendants since at least 1817. It remained as the Punch Inn for sixty years, latterly as a Worthington's house, and was closed on 12th February 1927.

The site was rebuilt as housing in the late 1980s.

SECTION 2: THE SOUTH MYTON AREA

SOUTH MYTON AREA: LOCATION MAP

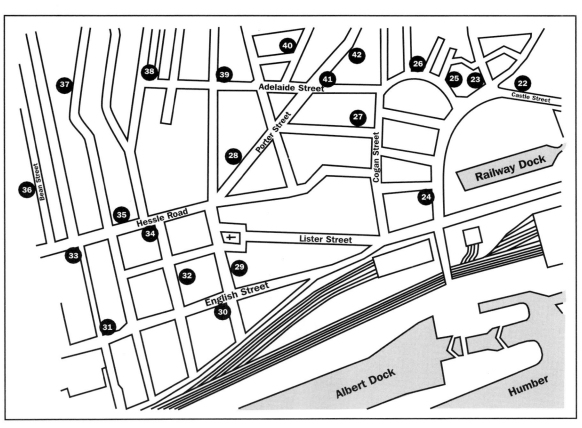

22. REGATTA TAVERN, CASTLE STREET
23. ROBIN HOOD HOTEL, MYTON PLACE
24. ALBERT DOCK HOTEL, COMMERCIAL ROAD
25. THREE TUNS INN, GREAT PASSAGE STREET
26. MARLBOROUGH HOTEL, GREAT PASSAGE STREET
27. ALEXANDRA INN, WILLIAM STREET
28. PORTLAND ARMS, PORTER STREET
29. PRINCE OF WALES, ST JAMES' STREET
30. WEST DOCK HOTEL, ENGLISH STREET
31. CORPORATION ARMS, NEPTUNE STREET
32. WESTERN TAVERN, ALFRED STREET
33. LILY HOTEL, HESSLE ROAD
34. THE ROSE TAVERN, HESSLE ROAD
35. SHEFFIELD ARMS, HESSLE ROAD
36. ENGINEERS ARMS, BEAN STREET
37. RISING SUN HOTEL, CAMPBELL STREET
38. ALBANY HOTEL, DAY STREET
39. ALBERT HOTEL, ADELAIDE STREET
40. BARREL TAVERN, HILL STREET
41. MYTON TAVERN, PORTER STREET
42. LEEDS ARMS, PORTER STREET

22. REGATTA TAVERN, CASTLE STREET

The Regatta Tavern at No. 8 Castle Street was originally the office and home of Thomas & Robert Boyes, merchants and Hanoverian Consul. They were listed in the 1817 trade directory as occupying No. 8 Castle Street, and as can be seen from the picture the building was formerly a house.

By the 1840s Francis Welburn, a tailor, formerly in business at No. 4 Castle Street, became a beer retailer at No. 8. Set back from the main road, the building was in fact inside Smiths Place, a small alley at the side of the Earl De Grey public house.

It must have proved a popular establishment because at closure in January 1925 £2300 compensation was paid to the owners. The building survived as the Regatta Cafe and eventually closed during the 1960s.

23. ROBIN HOOD HOTEL, MYTON PLACE

The Robin Hood or Robin Hood & Little John as it had also been known, opened at the end of the 18th century as a wine & spirit stores at No.11 Myton Place. In 1803 Richard Hall was listed in the local trade directory as victualler at the Robin Hood, Myton Place.

The original building would have enjoyed quite a rural location within Myton at that time, surrounded by windmills, gardens and a few grand houses and, as yet, no western docks. The 1908 Kingston upon Hull Myton Street Improvement Scheme affected the original building. The street was widened, straightened and the south end rounded off.

The owners, the Hull Brewery Co., built the new pub on the corner very near to its original site where it remained until demolition 60 years later in 1968.

24. ALBERT DOCK HOTEL, COMMERCIAL ROAD

Hull's Albert Dock was opened in July 1869, and near the east end of the new dock was a road known as Castle Row. Castle Row was widened and straightened to accommodate the increase in trade from the western docks and re-named Commercial Road, reflecting the nature of the area. These alterations required the demolition of the old Dock Green School at the corner of Edward's Place.

The Albert Dock Hotel was built on the new corner and enjoyed prime position in what was an extremely busy area. The entrance to the dock was at the south end of Commercial Road and thousands of workers must have passed the Albert and its near neighbour the Whittington Inn on their way to and from work.

The Hull Brewery Co. closed the pub on 15th October 1959 and the site has since been re-developed as the Kingston Retail Park.

25. THREE TUNS INN, GREAT PASSAGE STREET

Great Passage Street was originally a simple back way to the grand 18th century houses of Marine Row, which faced south across the River Humber. Following large scale property development at the beginning of the 19th century thousands of small, sub-standard cottages and courtyard houses were built in the area.

The Three Tuns was erected at this time and in 1826 J.Leake was recorded as probably the first licensee of the Three Tuns, No.16 Gt. Passage Street.

The pub thrived for many years amongst this densely populated working class area but following large-scale demolition and the subsequent loss of trade the Three Tuns closed in March 1936.

Its name and licence, along with the licence of the Oxford in North Street was passed to a new public house on Boothferry Road, which was also to be known as the Three Tuns.

26. MARLBOROUGH HOTEL, GREAT PASSAGE STREET

The Marlborough Hotel was first known as the 'Grapes', one of the most common names for a drinking establishment and one of at least a dozen in Hull in the first years of the 19th century.

It held a prominent position at the junction with Lower Union Street, which can be seen from this picture showing the Marlborough photographed by the Hull Brewery Co. in the 1920s. Inside Lower Union Street can be seen the former Wesleyan Mission room which opened in 1882, which became an Independent Methodist Chapel in 1911 and later St. Victor's Undenominational Chapel.

Both buildings were demolished circa 1968-69 following the compulsory purchase of the whole of the south side of Osborne Street.

27. ALEXANDRA INN, WILLIAM STREET

William Street took its name from King William IV who reigned from 1830 to 1837, a period when large parts of this area of the town were being developed.

The Alexandra Inn was a typical small beer house converted from a shop, and stood on the north side of the street. Edward Preston had been a beer retailer at the Earl Cardigan, Fish Street, in 1834. He moved to this newly developed area of the town in 1835 and set up shop as a coal merchant and grocer before becoming a beer retailer circa 1840. He may have named the pub in honour of Princess Alexandra of Denmark who in 1863 married Albert Edward, Prince of Wales.

Originally belonging to John Hunt's brewery of nearby Waverley Street, the freehold was acquired by the Hull Brewery Co. in the 1890s.

The Alexandra Inn survived for over 100 years until its closure in 1947.

28. PORTLAND ARMS, PORTER STREET

Confusion has surrounded the two drinking establishments situated in Porter Street with the name Portland Arms. The 'Original Portland Arms' was situated on the east side at No.123, and the one shown in this photograph, originally a beer-house named the Golden Ball, occupied No.136 on the west side.

By 1901, when it was purchased by Moors' & Robinson's, number 136 had become the Portland Arms. The frontage shown in the photograph was added by the brewery in 1913. The west side of Porter Street was due for redevelopment when this picture was taken in the 1930s and the Portland Arms is shown in this photograph as being 'To Let'. The large brick building next to the pub was the bottle store of ale & porter merchants T.Linsley & Co., formerly the site of Kendall & Gruby's 'Exchange Brewery'.

The pub was damaged during the Second World War when this side of Porter Street was blitzed.

29. PRINCE OF WALES, ST JAMES' STREET

The Prince of Wales at Nos.37-39 St.James' Street was a simple beer house whose original ownership is unclear. A George Smith became a beer retailer in 1834 and may have been the first victualler of the Prince of Wales.

The name Martin H. Cross etched into the window glass, refers to Martin Henry Cross, who owned a brewery in Osbourne Street. Cross's brewery was taken over by Gleadow & Dibb in 1887 and subsequently became part of the Hull Brewery Co.

The pub was very popular throughout its life with many workers from the engineering factories and railway yards along English Street. The Prince of Wales ceased trading almost 130 years after opening, finally closing on 1st August 1960 when the licence was transferred to the Albion Hotel, Caroline Street.

30. WEST DOCK HOTEL, ENGLISH STREET

The West Dock Hotel, English Street, was first recorded at the beginning of the 19th century as the Baltic Tavern. One of the first recorded victuallers was John Griffin in 1803, who had a short tenure due to his early death.

The Hull Advertiser newspaper of the 14th July 1804 carried an announcement for an auction to take place "at the house of the Widow Griffin known by the sign of the Ship and commonly called the Baltic Tavern". Following the announcement of a proposed new dock west of the town during the 1860s the Baltic Tavern changed its name to the West Dock Hotel.

The pub was one of the Hessle Road's most popular drinking houses and was known to the local inhabitants as 'Pops' after Thomas Poppleton, a very popular licensee from the 1930s to the 1950s.

31. CORPORATION ARMS, NEPTUNE STREET

The Corporation Arms stood at the junction of Neptune Street and English Street and opened in the 1870s, and was one of several public houses that once served this area. The licence came from the former Corporation Arms, Wellington Street, which closed in the 1860s for the works associated with the new West Dock (Albert Dock).

The pub was latterly known to the residents of the area as 'Chester's', after the popular Chester family who were licensees of several public houses in west Hull and ran the Corporation Arms 'on and off' for around fifty years.

The pub was demolished in preparation for the expansion of the T.J. Smith & Nephew factories during the late 1960s and early 1970s.

32. WESTERN TAVERN, ALFRED STREET

The Western Tavern was known at the beginning of the 19th century as the Gate Inn. Following re-fronting around 1860 the Gate Inn became the Western Tavern. The pub seems to have suffered as a direct consequence of being immediately next door to the more popular Inkerman Tavern which resulted in its closure on 12th February 1927.

The Hull Brewery Co. was paid £1000 in compensation for the 'extinguishment of the licence' and the site was sold to Moors' & Robson's, the owners of the Inkerman Tavern. Both houses were demolished and a new building was erected on the site, which took in the whole corner of Alfred Street and Edgar Street. This new building retained the name Inkerman Tavern, which it does to this day.

33. LILY HOTEL, HESSLE ROAD

The Lily Hotel stood at No.91 Hessle Road at the corner of Neptune Street. In 1846 Thomas Wheatley, ginger beer manufacturer, was living at No.1 Neptune Street. His business was enlarged by his son William during the 1870s at which point he opened a beer house on the site naming it the Lily Hotel.

The Lily received its first full licence on the 2nd March 1953 when it took the suspended licence of the Windsor, Waterworks Street, which had been destroyed during the blitz of May 1941.

The Lily was demolished circa 1969-70 following the compulsory purchase of the property in the area, which also claimed the nearby Rose Tavern and Foundry Arms.

34. THE ROSE TAVERN, HESSLE ROAD

The Rose appears to have first opened during the 1860s. Situated at the north end of Alfred Street, it was recorded as a licensed ale & porter store run by Dennis Taylor, the licensee of the nearby Sheffield Arms.

Towards the end of the 19th century various terraces on the south side of the Hessle Road were rebuilt on a much larger scale than the original single-storey buildings. The Rose was altered during this re-development, to take in the entire corner of Alfred Street. Originally a beer-only house, it was not granted a full licence until the 5th February 1959 when the licence of the Shoulder of Mutton, Lime Street was surrendered.

The Rose was demolished circa 1969/70 following a compulsory purchase order for the area that also required the demolition of the Lily Hotel and Foundry Arms.

35. SHEFFIELD ARMS, HESSLE ROAD

The Sheffield Arms was opened on the north side of the Hessle Road at the beginning of the 1850s when a Dennis Taylor was shown as a beer retailer at No.68. This small beer house probably occupied a former grocer's shop, situated in the middle of the row of terraced property between Campbell Street and Staniforth Place.

This picture taken by the Hull Brewery Co. in the 1920s shows the Sheffield Arms to have been re-built, enlarged and re-fronted with green glazed bricks and tiles. A nice feature of the decoration was its name Sheffield Arms in raised letter tiles above the central entrance door, some of which were saved at the time of its closure in the 1960s.

36. ENGINEERS ARMS, BEAN STREET

Bean Street was not shown on the 1853 Ordnance Survey plan of Hull but had been almost fully developed by 1875. The Engineers Arms was probably purpose built as a beer-house and stood at the south end of Bean Street on the corner of Wilberforce Terrace. Bean Street was very long and contained many terraces of houses but surprisingly only two pubs, the other being the Bean Hotel at the north end.

The beer-house was primarily a Bass & Co. establishment but the fine enamel sign above the door of the 'ale & porter store' notes that it also stocked bottles of Barclay, Perkins & Co. Celebrated London Stout (in Imperial Pints at 2/6d per dozen).

Its position in the centre of such a densely populated working class district enabled the Engineers Arms to thrive, and later to enlarge by acquiring the adjoining property. It remained open for almost 100 years before finally closing in the 1960s.

37. RISING SUN HOTEL, CAMPBELL STREET

Campbell Street was laid out circa 1860 and this beer-house, later named the Rising Sun Inn opened shortly after. It stood at No.98 Campbell Street on the corner of Studley Terrace and was converted from two small houses.

A valuation of the assets of the Hull Brewery Co. in 1890 valued the Rising Sun Hotel, as it had become known, at £2500. The arched entrance to the right of the pub in this photograph of circa 1925 led to the stores of John Harold Longbottom, one of a large family of greengrocers in the area.

The pub closed in August 1962 during widespread redevelopment of the area and the licence was transferred to a new pub, which was also to be known as the Rising Sun, Beverley High Road.

38. ALBANY HOTEL, DAY STREET

The Albany Hotel was first opened in January 1874 when the licence from the Pilot Boy Tavern, situated at the south end of Neptune Street, was transferred following closure. The enlargement of the railway network then taking place alongside the docks had required its demolition.

The Albany was for a brief time a beer-only house but soon became a fully licensed freehold house belonging to the wine & spirit merchants Willford & McBride, who owned several public houses in West Hull.

Before and after the Second World War the pub was known by locals as 'Crossey's' a reference to John Cross, a popular licensee from the 1930s. The pub closed circa 1966/67 and was demolished during the large-scale redevelopment of the area.

39. ALBERT HOTEL, ADELAIDE STREET

The Albert Hotel received its licence after the closure of the Bath Tavern, Humber Bank in 1850. This 'Albert' was one of several establishments named in honour of Prince Albert who opened the Great Exhibition of 1851.

Its first licensee, Joseph Wharam, was also a brassfounder and gas-fitter but by 1863 Joseph's wife Ann Wharam was named as the holder of the licence. Living at the same address from 1863 was a Robert Wharam, brewer and licensed victualler of the Myton Tavern in nearby Porter Street. Robert ran a small brewery at the rear of the Albert Hotel, previously occupied by Robert Hesp. Robert Wharam's son (Robert junior) also became a businessman, later having a hairdressers and tobacconist shop at No.66 Porter Street.

The Albert Hotel closed on the 22nd August 1949 and its licence was transferred to a new pub to be named the Bridges on Sutton Road.

40. BARREL TAVERN, HILL STREET

The Barrel Tavern was a typical late Victorian beer-house, which like many of the period had only a relatively short life. Converted from a private house at No.32 Hill Street in the 1880s it remained open for around 25 years and was converted back to a house circa 1916 when many back street pubs were being closed. The large arch seen to the right of the Barrel Tavern led to houses in Furniture Place.

Many beer-houses had been converted from ordinary dwelling houses or small shops following the implementation of the 1830 Beer House Act. In 1916 the pub was referred to the Licensing (Compensation) Committee under the Licensing (Consolidation) Act 1910 and placed on the redundancy list. The owners objected to the closure and complained of the loss of revenue claiming £1280 in compensation for their loss.

41. MYTON TAVERN, PORTER STREET

The Myton Tavern at No.61 Porter Street was a Hull Brewery Co. beer-house which opened during the 1840s. The street was numbered sequentially at this time and the beer house was originally No.28, situated at the junction with Adelaide Street.

The Myton Tavern maintained good trade throughout its life and was noted for its large clock above the curved corner. Following large-scale slum clearance in the area during the 1930s the pub stood isolated, only to be closed after sustaining damage following an air raid on 8th May 1941.

Before closure the Myton Tavern was known as 'Freddie Fox's', another west Hull pub which retained the name of a popular licensee from the 1930s. The licence was then held in suspension until 1951 when it was transferred to the Mayberry, Maybury Road.

42. LEEDS ARMS, PORTER STREET

To the left of this 1940s photograph of Porter Street is the Darley's beer-house known as the Leeds Arms. The Leeds Arms, which originally dated from the 1850s, was rebuilt around 1936 and this is the building shown here.

The property suffered during the Blitz of 1941, having its windows blown out on several occasions, but was relatively lucky to sustain little structural damage.

Having survived the Blitz and in its modernised form it became the last remaining building along this section of Porter Street, before finally being demolished in 1958.

SECTION 3: NORTH MYTON AND BEYOND

NORTH MYTON AND BEYOND: LOCATION MAP

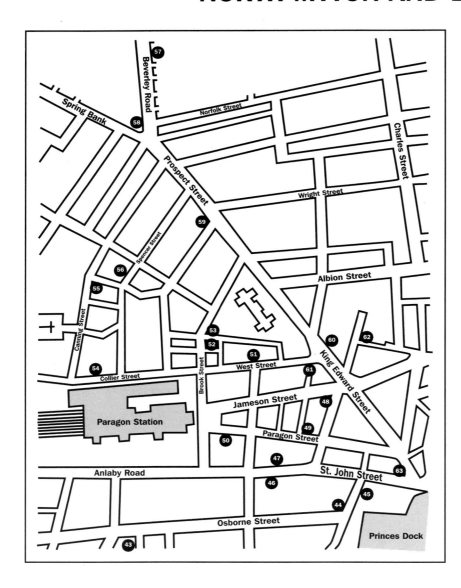

43. DRUM & CYMBALS, OSBORNE STREET
44. NORWOOD ARMS, OSBORNE STREET
45. PUNCH HOTEL, WATERHOUSE LANE
46. OLD BLACK HORSE HOTEL, CARR LANE
47. WHITE HORSE HOTEL, CARR LANE
48. GOLDEN BALL, CHARIOT STREET
49. BRUNSWICK HOTEL, PARAGON STREET
50. TALBOT INN, PARAGON STREET
51. STAR OF THE WEST, WEST STREET
52. STATION HOTEL, MIDDLE STREET
53. GRAPES INN, BROOK STREET
54. WHITE LION INN, COLLIER STREET
55. CARTMAN'S ARMS, CANNING STREET
56. BEVERLEY ARMS, SPENCER STREET
57. SWAN INN, BEVERLEY ROAD
58. ZOOLOGICAL HOTEL, BEVERLEY ROAD
59. OXFORD INN, NORTH STREET
60. WHEATSHEAF HOTEL, KING EDWARD STREET
61. ROSE & CROWN INN, WEST STREET
62. BOWLING GREEN TAVERN, WALTHAM STREET
63. QUEEN'S ARMS, JUNCTION STREET & ST. JOHN STREET

43. DRUM & CYMBALS, OSBORNE STREET

This pub building was not mentioned as a beer-house until the 1860s when Charles Harrop was listed as a beer retailer at No.107 Osborne Street. It is interesting to note that it was one of ten 'pubs' in the street in 1867. By 1874 it was recorded as the Drum & Cymbals for the first time. The Hull Brewery Co. later acquired the premises circa 1887.

Showing a remarkable resemblance to the Lockwood Arms (now the Bull & Bush) on Green Lane, the Drum & Cymbals shown in this photograph is a re-fronted version of circa 1916.

It stood at the corner of Upper Union Street and Osborne Street until its closure in 1956, when the licence was surrendered for the granting of a full licence to the Old English Gentleman in Worship Street. The building was demolished circa 1958/9.

44. NORWOOD ARMS, OSBORNE STREET

Charles Morgan Norwood, a local shipping magnate, was elected as one of two Liberal MPs for Hull in 1865 and was a staunch temperance man. It is therefore unlikely that a public house would be named in his honour, so it is more likely that the name was a side-swipe at his temperance leanings.

A typical Victorian conversion of a former shop, No.2 Osborne Street had been a butcher's shop in 1863 but by the mid-1860s it was recorded as a beer-house known as the Norwood Arms.

The Norwood suffered from very stiff competition in the area and following severe damage during the Blitz, its licence was placed in suspension in 1942, eventually being surrendered in 1957 to grant a full licence to the Dairycoates Inn on Hessle Road.

45. PUNCH HOTEL, WATERHOUSE LANE

To the rear of the present Punch Hotel in Queen Victoria Square is the site of the original Punch of circa 1845, which fronted Waterhouse Lane (a section which is now lost beneath the entrance to the Princes Quay shopping complex). The Hull Advertiser newspaper published a description of the 'new' Punch Hotel, on the 16th October 1846.

The re-development of the area around St. John Street and Waterworks Street at the turn of the century gave an opportunity to relocate the Punch to a more prominent position.

In 1894/5 the old Punch was demolished and rebuilt in its present form to the designs of architects Smith, Brodrick & Lowther, re-opening in 1896.

46. OLD BLACK HORSE HOTEL, CARR LANE

Almost as old as Carr Lane itself, the Black Horse had stood on the south side of the street since at least 1790. In the Hull trade directory of 1791 Timothy Reeves, a brewer, was listed as victualler at the Black Horse Inn.

The original building would have appeared very similar to the White Horse on the opposite side of the street. The grand building shown in this photograph is a later rebuild of the 19th century.

To the left of the Black Horse can be seen the edge of the Grosvenor Hotel. Both buildings suffered severe damage following bombing on the 24th November 1941 and were subsequently demolished. Following the air-raid there was a special removal of its licence to a former shop at No.6 Porter Street, and with the transfer of the licence the new premises also took the name Old Black Horse.

47. WHITE HORSE HOTEL, CARR LANE

The land on which the original inn stood was recorded as early as the 15th century as 'White Horse Ings'. As Hull grew beyond the walls of the old town in the 18th century the main route to the west was Carr Lane. From its earliest days many inns were dotted along this route, one of which became known as the White Horse.

Originally a large coaching inn it had stabling for at least sixty horses. The original buildings, dating from the middle of the 18th century, survived until the 1950s. These included the arched entrance to the stables and some of the stables themselves.

The old unfashionable structure was demolished and rebuilt in typically sparse fashion, generously described at the time as Neo-Georgian. The new White Horse re-opened in December 1956. This 1940s photograph shows part of the old property.

48. GOLDEN BALL, CHARIOT STREET

Although never quite sure whether it was in Chariot Street or Carlisle Street, this turn of the century photograph of the Golden Ball shows it to have been the epitome of a small purpose built Victorian beer-house.

The Hull burgess roll for 1865-66 listed Edward Gallagher at No.23 Chariot Street and in 1867 No. 23 was listed in a trade directory as a beer-house, victualler Mr.E.Gallagher. From 1876 it was named as the 'Golden Ball'.

The construction of the final section of Jameson Street commenced early in 1901 and required the demolition of the northern end of Chariot Street, which included the Golden Ball and by 1902 it ceased to be listed in any records.

49. BRUNSWICK HOTEL, PARAGON STREET

The building that later became the Brunswick Hotel was originally built circa 1815. It was mentioned in the census return of 1851 when Joseph Schofield, aged 40, was listed as Innkeeper at the 'Railway Tavern', Paragon Street. The pub had been named following the construction of the Paragon Station circa 1847. The Railway Tavern became the Brunswick Tavern circa 1887.

The Brunswick was one of only two properties that survived on this section of Paragon Street during the Blitz. This photograph shows the pub shortly after the war, in 1949. Following the devastation in the area the site was redeveloped as the Queens House buildings in 1953. The 'Old Brunswick' was demolished and rebuilt a few yards further north in Chapel Street.

The new building is still in use as a pub and is now known as the Bass House.

50. TALBOT INN, PARAGON STREET

The building that became the Talbot Inn was built circa 1860 and the first recorded victualler was William Ibbetson, who was recorded as a "beer-house keeper" in the 1871 Census. The name Talbot was taken from a large type of hunting dog.

In 1872 the single roomed dram shop was altered to a larger two-roomed beer-house and in 1927 Quibell & Son reconstructed the simple shop front of the Talbot in typical Art Deco style. A fine Moors' & Robson's sign board hung above the first floor window as shown in this photograph of circa 1955.

The Talbot only recently lost its identity and became the Stonehouse when it was extended to take in property next door. Today it has been refurbished again and is a 1970s theme bar known as Flares - and so qualifies as one of Hull's lost pubs.

51. STAR OF THE WEST, WEST STREET

Still fresh in the memory of most Hull drinking folk, the Star of the West began life as a three-storey house of circa 1780 with a front garden. The name may have been a sea-faring reference, as a large portion of its custom would have come from the many mariners in lodgings around the area. The area was also referred to as the 'West End' and this may have been another inspiration for its name.

Following the pattern of most of its neighbours it became a shop in the early part of the 19th century and then a small beer house. The photograph clearly shows how it extended over its garden as a single storey shop typical of its period in the 1860s. Following its continued success the front buildings were later built upon and the Star of the West acquired the more familiar imitation half-timbered façade in 1926.

The pub was demolished in 1997 for the proposed extension to the Prospect Centre shopping complex.

52. STATION HOTEL, MIDDLE STREET

An inn of some kind had stood on this site since the 1820s, when it was known as the Golden Ball, 27 Middle Street. Between 1840 and 1842 the Golden Ball became the Acorn and by 1882 it was listed as the Dublin Hotel.

Brook Street had been extended south to provide better access to Paragon Station in the 1880s and the new alignment meant the Dublin was now on the corner of both Brook Street and Middle Street.

This photograph shows the rebuilt Dublin complete with 'Harp' decoration in the eaves. The Irish link was strong in this area, which had always been heavily populated with Irish immigrant workers.

By 1915 the Dublin had changed its name for the final time to the Station Hotel which it remained until closure on 12th June 1958. The site is now within the C&A store on Ferensway.

53. GRAPES INN, BROOK STREET

This photograph was taken by a member of the Hull Photographic Society in 1926 and shows the Grapes Inn on the east side of Brook Street at its junction with Mill Street. The lettering on the signboard shows that the inn was also known as the 'West End Wine & Spirit Vaults' when the photograph was taken, although it had been known as the Grapes since at least 1820.

In the background are the three storey buildings of the Watts Nurses Homes, which were to the rear of the Infirmary on Prospect Street and the large chimney of the boilerhouse of the Infirmary laundry.

The construction of Ferensway in the early 1930s had a direct effect on the pub, which was almost totally demolished and reconstructed as the Broadway Hotel circa 1933. The Mill Street entrance of the Grapes can be directly related to the side door of the Broadway, which is now known as Mr.Q's.

54. WHITE LION INN, COLLIER STREET

Collier Street (originally Collier's Street) was laid out circa 1830 on land at the end of West Street purchased by Joseph Collier. By 1835 John Wass a builder and victualler had opened the Bricklayer's Arms at No.41 Collier Street.

The name was an obvious reference to his trade and perhaps that of many of his customers. Cheap property was being built at an incredible rate in this area at the time and many bricklayers would have found work in the area.

Around 1875 its name changed to the White Lion and it was probably at this point that the building was rebuilt as shown in this photograph of circa 1925.

Following the development of the corporation bus station the White Lion was demolished and relocated further north in the summer of 1934, on land which had been cleared for the Ferensway development.

55. CARTMAN'S ARMS, CANNING STREET

The Cartman's Arms became a beer-house shortly after the Beer-house Act of 1830, which enabled almost anyone who could afford the two guinea licence fee to open premises for the sale of beer and cider. It was listed from around 1834 in the trade directories and was situated at the corner of Canning Street and Booth Street.

A Hull Brewery Co. pub for most of its latter years, it was extended from one house to include the three premises shown in this photograph of circa 1925.

The pub closed in November 1931, a casualty of the wide-scale redevelopment of the area.

56. BEVERLEY ARMS, SPENCER STREET

Spencer Street was in an area of very low quality housing to the west of Ferensway and was home to many immigrant communities.

The pub was first mentioned in the 1820s as a beer-house at No.36 Spencer Street. The construction of Ferensway and the associated building works in the early 1930s required the demolition of much of the property in the area. The Beverley Arms was situated on the west side of Spencer Street and its site was under the recently demolished corporation bus shed on what is currently known as Lombard Street. The final victualler was former wrestling and weightlifting champion Tommy Bilham who had the house until its closure in 1932.

57. SWAN INN, BEVERLEY ROAD

This photograph shows the Swan Inn prior to its rebuilding in 1898. It had originally been a house with front garden and in the same way as the Star of the West on West Street it extended by building a 'bar' room over its front garden.

It appears to have been first listed in 1876 when Joseph Nattriss was a beer retailer at 12 North Parade, Beverley Road. By the 1880s it became known as the Swan Inn and in 1898 the now familiar frontage of the Swan appeared as part of a major rebuild by a Mr. Goates, costing £1,094.

It was granted a full 7-day licence on surrender of the licences of the Foresters Arms, Finkle Street, and the Flying Horse, Sewer Lane, in 1900.

The Swan had also been recorded as the Swann Inn on a number of occasions but which is correct is a mystery, although there was at one time a beer retailer in Hull with the name Swann. Oblivious to the mystery surrounding its name, the current Swan continues to serve the public of Beverley Road.

58. ZOOLOGICAL HOTEL, BEVERLEY ROAD

Although of an earlier date, the inn that became the Zoological was mentioned in the Hull Advertiser newspaper in July 1815 as "Mrs Dunn, sign of the Ship". The trade directory of 1823 confirmed a Mrs. Ann Dunn as the victualler of the Ship Inn, Beverley Road. Around 1840 the Ship became known as the Zoological Hotel, not surprisingly this was also the date of the opening of the Zoological Gardens on Spring Bank.

The pub was a favourite of Hull's drinking fraternity and a Hull Brewery Co. house for most of its latter years and many locals enjoyed its last night on 2nd March 1985.

The Hull Daily Mail complex at Blundell's Corner now occupies the site.

59. OXFORD INN, NORTH STREET

North Street was laid out on the west side of Prospect Street in the late 18th century. Thomas Wardell was one of the earliest victuallers of a beer-house at No.2 North Street, and is mentioned in trade directories from the 1830s. The house later became known as the Oxford Inn. It was originally of three bays but the property later extended west over vacant land to create an extra bar.

Shown on this photograph to the right of the Oxford are the premises of Bladon's the drapers, whose main entrance was in Prospect Street. Following closure in 1936 the licence of the Oxford was transferred along with the licence of the Three Tuns, Great Passage Street, for the granting of a full licence to the new Three Tuns, Boothferry Road.

60. WHEATSHEAF HOTEL, KING EDWARD STREET

A windmill had stood on the site, which is now the corner of King Edward Street and Waltham Street, since at least 1652, and it is likely that an inn would also have been nearby. This inn later became known as the Mill and by 1822 had become the Wheatsheaf Inn (although also known as the Wheelrights' Arms for a short time).

The building line was set back slightly during the construction of King Edward Street in 1901, which necessitated the reconstruction of the front of the Wheatsheaf.

The oil painting of a sheaf of wheat, which had hung outside, was replaced by a similar design in ceramic tiles within the entrance of the new building. Having survived both World Wars the Wheatsheaf was suddenly demolished in February 1973.

61. ROSE & CROWN INN, WEST STREET

West Street was constructed at the end of the 18th century and William Blackeston was listed in the 1803 trade directory as one of the first victuallers of the Rose & Crown at No. 1.

An entry to the left of the front window led to the rear rooms of the inn which included a Smoke Room and a Dining Room which had previously been the 'tap room'. This passage also gave access to the north end of Chapel Street.

The tap-room was originally part of the large brewery buildings of the Hopwood family, which survived behind the Rose & Crown until the construction of Jameson Street in 1901.

The Rose & Crown survived until 8th July 1930 when it was officially closed.

62. BOWLING GREEN TAVERN, WALTHAM STREET

Waltham Street was named after the 18th century businessman Thomas Waltham, owner of the windmill that had stood on the land for many decades if not centuries and latterly known as Waltham Mill.

On the south side of Waltham Street had been a bowling green which gave its name to Bowling Green Court, which in turn gave its name to the Bowling Green Tavern circa 1820. As this photograph shows, the tavern's entrances were both within the narrow court, which led to Little Albion Street and Davis Street.

By 1930 trade was in decline as the pub was off the main road and much of the area was being demolished following compulsory purchase, which resulted in the tavern's closure during the 1930s.

63. QUEEN'S ARMS, JUNCTION STREET & ST. JOHN STREET

Prior to the building of the City Hall two large blocks of property stood on the site and extended to within yards of the Dock Offices (now the Hull Maritime Museum). Following the erection of the Wilberforce Monument in 1834 at the point now known as Monument Bridge, a beer-house opened at the corner opposite and was named the Monument Tavern, victualler Mr. G. Weddell-Headley.

Following the accession of Queen Victoria in 1837, Mr. Weddell-Headley changed the name to the Queen's Arms Inn.

After the demolition of the property for the City Hall development, the licence of the Queen was transferred to the bar of the City Hall itself. It is interesting to note that a public house named the Queen once stood on the site now occupied by the statue of Queen Victoria in what is now Queen Victoria Square.

SECTION 4: THE SCULCOATES AREA

THE SCULCOATES AREA: LOCATION MAP

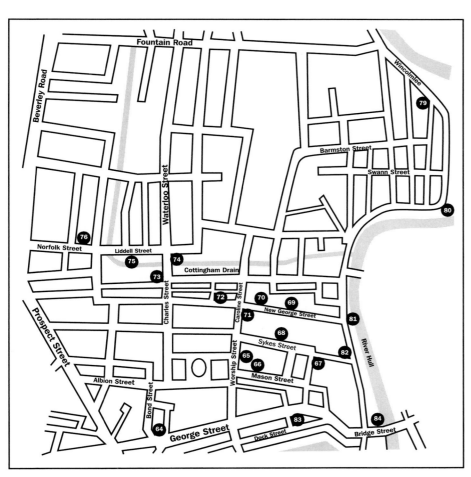

64. KING WILLIAM IV INN, BOND STREET
65. STAR INN, WORSHIP STREET
66. LORD RAGLAN INN, MASON STREET
67. SUN INN, BOURNE STREET
68. GRAPES INN, SYKES STREET
69. BARREL TAVERN, NEW GEORGE STREET
70. MILTON TAVERN, NEW GEORGE STREET
71. SHAKESPEARE TAVERN, CAROLINE STREET
72. LION INN, FRANCIS STREET EAST
73. SCULCOATES ARMS, CHARLES STREET
74. BURN'S HEAD, WATERLOO STREET
75. MECHANICS' ARMS, LIDDELL STREET
76. DOVER CASTLE INN, NORFOLK STREET
77. HORSE CLIPPERS' ARMS, AIR STREET *not shown on map
78. GOLDEN BALL INN, AIR STREET *not shown on map
79. OLD GREENLAND FISHERY INN, WINCOLMLEE
80. FERRY BOAT TAVERN, WINCOLMLEE
81. SCULCOATES HOTEL, WINCOLMLEE
82. DE LA POLE TAVERN, WINCOLMLEE
83. BLACK SWAN INN, DOCK STREET
84. GREENLAND FISHERY, CHARLOTTE STREET

64. KING WILLIAM IV INN, BOND STREET

The Bond Street we know today is very different from the original Bond Street, which occupied only the west side of the present dual carriageway. In the centre of the block of property occupying the south end of the street stood the King William IV pub.

First known as the White Horse, one of its first victuallers was Charles Murgatroyd in 1803. During its life it was also known as the King, the Kings Head and the King William.

One can only imagine how the original building would have looked; this photograph of the early 1950s shows the pub prior to its closure and demolition in 1957 for the redevelopment of Bond Street.

Its licence was transferred along with that of the pub latterly known as the 'Tally Ho', which had stood opposite since circa 1800, to the new Viking pub on Shannon Road.

65. STAR INN, WORSHIP STREET

The Star Inn stood directly opposite the entrance to the yard of the present Central Fire Station in Worship Street, and was a simple one-room inn first recorded as a beer-house around 1876, when the beer retailer was J. Ward.

The door on the left of this 1920's photograph led to housing at rear of the property, known as Chapel Court. Chapel Court had been named after the Tabernacle Independent Chapel, which opened in 1827 on the corner of Worship Street and Sykes Street.

Stiff competition in the area spelt the end for the smallest pub in the street. Within a few hundred yards there were at least a dozen drinking establishments. The Star Inn closed on the 19th January 1934 and reverted to its original form as a dwelling house.

66. LORD RAGLAN INN, MASON STREET

The building partly obscured by the tree to the left of this photograph had obviously been a pub at some time. No doubt the locals seated on the bench would have some memories of the Lord Raglan Inn, which had stood at No.9 Mason Street since the street was laid out at the end of the 18th century. The house was one of many to open following the 'Beer-House Act' of 1830 and one of the earliest recorded victuallers was a Sarah Bailey in 1834. A later victualler, William Jacks, also had a licence to run Hackney Carriages from the premises during the 1830s.

The building was re-fronted just before the First World War and survived until 1934 when the premises were closed and the licence transferred along with that of the Talbot, Scale Lane, for a new pub, the Hastings, on Spring Bank West. The buildings were demolished and the site is now the entrance to the Mason Street car park.

67. SUN INN, BOURNE STREET

This photograph shows the Sun Inn, which occupied the corner of Bourne Street and Charterhouse Lane. It was first recorded as a beer-house around 1876 when the victualler was a Thomas Crowston.

The Moors' & Robson's Brewery Co. purchased the Sun Inn in 1892 for £1,200 and immediately carried out alterations to the exterior. Their painted advertisement can be seen on the Charterhouse Lane frontage in this photograph of circa 1930.

Following bomb damage in 1942, the Sun Inn was demolished and its licence suspended until 1953 when it was used to grant a full licence to the New Inn, Stoneferry. The site has remained undeveloped ever since.

68. GRAPES INN, SYKES STREET

In 1823 there were eight pubs named the Grapes in Hull and Richard Ward was listed at the Grapes, No.22 Sykes Street. Originally a very small inn, the Grapes was extended around 1830. These additions can be seen to the right of the original 3-storey building in this photograph of circa 1925 and included a small brewery and 'tap'.

To the right of the 'tap' can be seen the entrance to Mariners Court and to the left is the sunken terrace of houses with gardens known as Clarkes Square, a type of housing that was common in this area.

The Grapes was demolished circa 1926 and replaced by the new buildings, which remain to the present day. Sadly the owners have recently decided to re-name the pub and in doing so have removed the last 'Grapes' in Hull.

69. BARREL TAVERN, NEW GEORGE STREET

New George Street was laid out circa 1805-1810 and is thought to have been named after local landowner Sir George Pryme. This building on the north side of the street at the entrance to Nelson Square (which can be seen in this photograph) was opened as a beer-house in the 1820s and some years later it grew to take in the property to the west. An ornate bracket can be seen hanging above the main door and at one time may have had a barrel suspended from it.

The Barrel Tavern closed on the 17th April 1928 and its licence was transferred to the newly built Goodfellowship, Cottingham Road.

The pub was finally demolished in a slum clearance programme of the early 1930s.

70. MILTON TAVERN, NEW GEORGE STREET

It would be hard to find pub premises as small as this in modern Hull but at the time of this photograph, circa 1925, pubs of this size would still have been commonplace. Converted from a house around 1860, the Milton Tavern was enlarged with the addition of a smoke room to the rear of the building at the turn of the century. Prior to this the only room was the ornately-decorated bar with its corner door to New George Street.

The Milton's size was not the only reason for its demise; wide scale slum clearance from the 1920s resulted in most of the property in this area being demolished. The Milton closed circa 1928 and its licence was transferred along with that of the Barrel Tavern, also in New George Street, to the Goodfellowship on Cottingham Road.

71. SHAKESPEARE TAVERN, CAROLINE STREET

This building had been standing at the corner of Caroline Street and New George Street since the early 1820s. In a trade directory of 1855 it was listed as the premises of joiner and beer retailer Adam Killer.

The origin of its name is unknown although it could have been a reference to the nearby theatres on George Street, patrons of which may have passed the tavern on their way back to the railway station in Cannon Street if travelling by train.

The tavern survived until 1932 when it too was amongst the properties demolished under the slum clearance programme which cleared the way for the construction of the present housing in this area.

72. LION INN, FRANCIS STREET EAST

Built circa 1825 the Lion was first mentioned in a trade directory of 1863 as the Lion Tavern, run by beer retailer Mr. R. Beecroft. The Lion Inn had grown from its original corner house plot to take in other properties on Francis Street East following conversion from a house to a beer-house. It also had a 'bake house' at the rear along Christopher Street. Bakehouse was a term used to describe the brewing area of an inn rather than a bakery and these buildings can be seen in this photograph of circa 1925. Note the carved Lion guarding the door.

Following the demolition of the surrounding property during the 1930s and 1940s the Lion Inn along with its neighbour the Seedcrushers' Arms stood isolated for several years.

The Lion was finally demolished in the 1950s prior to the construction of the Clover Dairies warehouse and factory.

73. SCULCOATES ARMS, CHARLES STREET

Possibly one of the most attractive pub exteriors in Hull the loss of the 'Scully' was felt deeply by local historians and pub enthusiasts. It had been built between 1842 and 1848 and was shown on the large scale 1853 Ordnance Survey plan as the Sculcoates Inn.

The pub was refurbished in the 1890s when its famous ceramic-tiled exterior was added. Internally the Bar was finished in white glazed tiles and was out of bounds to women, who had to sit in the Snug entered by the side door in Raywell Street. It was run by Joseph Gorman for many years and was known locally as 'Smokey Joe's'. A long standing regular, Arthur Gibson recalls a brass bar ornament which had a permanently lit flame for smokers and a stove in the corner with a pan of peas sat warming on the top.

The pub closed on Sunday, April 9th 1972 but was not demolished until 1983.

74. BURN'S HEAD, WATERLOO STREET

This picture captures a moment in time during one summer morning in the 1950s. It shows the beginning of Waterloo Street at its junction with Richmond Terrace (known locally as 'Drainside').

On the corner of Richmond Terrace stood the Burn's Head, No.16 Richmond Terrace and 2 Waterloo Street, which was built circa 1850 and became a beer-house around 1851 when it was mentioned by name as the Burn's Head in the census of that year. By 1890 it had expanded to include the former butchers shop next door and around 1920 the old beer-house front was lost when the more fashionable Mock-Tudor black and white frontage was added.

The Burns Head was demolished in a compulsory purchase 'blitz' during 1972.

75. MECHANICS' ARMS, LIDDELL STREET

The Mechanics Arms was one of the first beer-houses to be built in the streets laid out on the lands of George Liddell.

Built between 1856 and 1863 possibly as a beer-house, it was first recorded in the trade directory of 1863 when Martha Turner-Ware was a beer retailer at No.41 Liddell Street, the corner of Richmond Terrace. To the right of this photograph is the Cottingham Drain, which ran under a bridge at this point (the junction between Liddell and Norfolk Street).

The tiled frontage included diamond shaped panels, each of which contained a hand-painted depiction of the various mechanics' skills. The Mechanics' name was a reference to the nearby Rose's foundry, situated in Cannon Street.

The pub was demolished circa 1972/3.

76. DOVER CASTLE INN, NORFOLK STREET

The original address of this beer-house at the corner of Russell Place, was No.1 Liddell Street, which originally began at this point and ran east to the junction with St.Paul's Street.

It was not shown on Wilkinson's plan of Hull in 1848 but was shown on the first Ordnance Survey plan of 1853. Plans of 1858 show it by name as the Dover Castle Inn.

By 1863 the beginning of Liddell Street had moved east and the Dover Castle's new address became No.39 Norfolk Street. In a breakdown of the Hull Brewery Co.'s assets in 1890 it was valued at £3,600 and was obviously a busy house.

A popular pub and one that retained its original name, it survived into the 1970s and was demolished under a compulsory purchase order of circa 1972-73.

77. HORSE CLIPPERS' ARMS, AIR STREET

It would come as a great surprise to most locals to learn that Air Street not only had the famous Golden Ball but two other pubs. The Tanners Arms was situated in Etherington's Place at the west end of the street and the Horse Clippers' Arms was directly opposite the Golden Ball.

Built as a dwelling house in the 1840s it had become a beer-house by 1872. In a trade directory of 1874 Thomas Kelswick was listed as a 'horse clipper' and by 1876 he was named as the victualler of the Horse Clippers Arms. Although not on the same scale as the Golden Ball but just as popular, it enjoyed good trade and was also a meeting place for one of the 'friendly societies', who used a club room to the rear of the property.

The Horse Clippers' closed in 1936 and suffered bomb damage in the Second World War. The ruined buildings were finally cleared in the 1950s.

78. GOLDEN BALL INN, AIR STREET

The Golden Ball had stood on the north side of Air Street to the west of the graveyard of the long demolished St. Mary's church since the end of the 18th century.

Joseph Tummins was one of the first recorded victuallers in 1810, when the pub was known as the Blue Ball. It stood alone initially and was later included in a small terrace named Eliza's Row. By 1882 it was known as the Golden Ball and in 1892 was purchased by the Hull Brewery Co. In a survey of the premises for the brewery in 1912 the auditor noted "good house-very little opposition".

Although much altered inside and out the pub always enjoyed excellent trade from the nearby factories and it came as a shock when it was sold and demolished for an extension to a factory yard in 1996.

79. OLD GREENLAND FISHERY INN, WINCOLMLEE

Converted from housing in the early 1820s the Greenland Fishery was recorded in the trade directory of 1823 when its address was No.27 Church Street, north of its junction with York Street. Its name was a reference to the Arctic whaling ships, many of which were built and sailed from the shipyards in the area.

The corner door led to the Bar and the next to the Smoke Room, which is marked on a sign in the window. Houses can be seen to the extreme right of the picture and the roof-line of the former Wincolmlee Primitive Methodist Chapel, which was built in 1842, all of which survive at the time of writing. However, the pub does not, having closed in 1933 when its licence was transferred along with that of the Railway Inn, Hedon Road to the new Endyke Hotel, Endike Lane.

80. FERRY BOAT TAVERN, WINCOLMLEE

This was one of the larger Wincolmlee pubs and started life as part of a row of dwelling houses situated to the south of the present Sculcoates Bridge, on the east side of Wincolmlee.

It became a beer-house in the 1840s and was known by the name Ferry Boat Tavern. Boats were used regularly around this area to transfer workers from the 'Groves' on the east side of the river to work in the factories on the west.

For a number of years during the 1870s it was known as Tiger No.5 as John Stephenson, landlord of Tiger No.1 in Waterworks Street had purchased several inns and given them all the name Tiger and a number. This was short-lived however and the pubs soon reverted to their original names.

The Ferry Boat Inn continued trading into the 1930s but on 17th December 1936 it closed for the last time and was later demolished.

81. SCULCOATES HOTEL, WINCOLMLEE

This was an interesting building located within warehouses on the east side of Wincolmlee, opposite the end of New George Street, with its back to the River Hull. It had been recorded as early as 1838 when a Daniel Maloney was the victualler.

Originally a Hunt's house, it was taken over by the Hull Brewery Co. in the 1880s.

In June 1937 the rear outbuildings, which had just been rebuilt following damage by a moored ship, collapsed into the river. The cause was given as subsidence due to erosion beneath the buildings and water entering the old cellars.

The remaining buildings survived the war and the pub continued trading until the late 50s. The site is now a business car park.

82. DE LA POLE TAVERN, WINCOLMLEE

At the east end of Charterhouse Lane at its junction with Wincolmlee stood the De La Pole Tavern. Buildings had stood at this corner since the middle of the 18th century and possibly earlier, and by 1803 the site had become a beer-house known as the Jug.

Following the widening of Wincolmlee circa 1840, the premises were rebuilt on a larger scale and named the De La Pole Tavern.

Along the north side of Charterhouse Lane can be seen the arched entrance to De La Pole Court and the old malt kiln of brewer's Brodrick & Peters who rented the property from the Charterhouse.

The Hull Brewery Co. took over the business in 1924 and this photograph is probably of that date. The tavern closed in 1933 and was later demolished.

83. BLACK SWAN INN, DOCK STREET

Dock Street was named after Hull's first dock of 1778, later Queens Dock, which was filled in during the 1930s and is now the Queens Gardens. The Black Swan stood at the corner of Princess Street (later Clifford Street) and Dock Street and was open by the early years of the 19th century.

It is difficult to imagine the site of the Black Swan in 1999, as the whole of this area was redeveloped in the early 1930s and then again in the 1980s for the construction of Freetown Way.

This photograph shows the Black Swan on the 1st August 1935. The pub closed following bomb damage on the 7th May 1941. The licence was suspended until December 1957 when it was transferred to the new Ganstead, Ganstead Lane, Bilton.

84. GREENLAND FISHERY, CHARLOTTE STREET

The name Greenland Fishery was a popular pub name around the banks of the River Hull. Historically the area had many 'Greenland' shipyards and whaling ships would have sailed from the many yards to join the Greenland fleet. Initially in Bridge Street which was laid out in 1791, the inn later became No.99 Charlotte Street when this section was re-named.

Situated on the north side of the street, it stood between the old North Bridge and Wincolmlee. It was recorded as early as 1803 by name as the Greenland Fishery when the victualler was a John Tennyson but it is very likely that an inn had stood at this site for many years prior; the building shown in this photograph could easily date from the end of the 18th century.

Following the opening of the present North Bridge in 1931 the property in the area was compulsorily purchased although these buildings survived until the late 1930s.

SECTION 5: EAST OF THE RIVER

EAST OF THE RIVER: LOCATION MAP

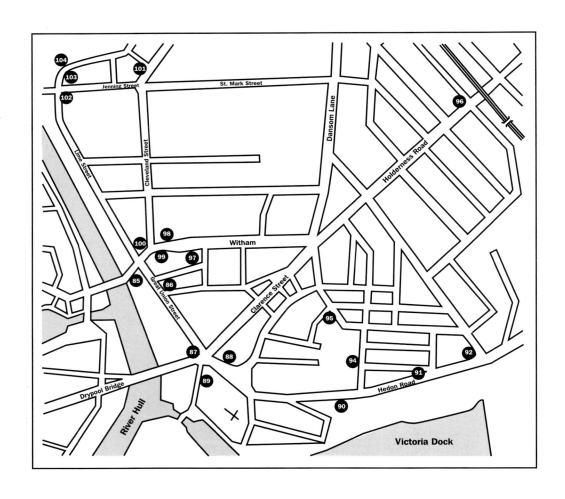

85. NORTH BRIDGE INN, WITHAM
86. CARPENTERS ARMS, GREAT UNION STREET
87. COMMERCIAL HOTEL, GREAT UNION STREET
88. ORDNANCE ARMS, GREAT UNION STREET
89. WATERLOO TAVERN, HARCOURT STREET
90. RAILWAY INN, HEDON ROAD
91. DOVER CASTLE HOTEL, HEDON ROAD
92. ALBION HOTEL, HEDON ROAD
93. ORIENTAL HOTEL, HEDON ROAD *not shown on map
94. BLUE BELL INN, THOMAS STREET
95. SHIPWRIGHT'S ARMS, MARVEL STREET
96. SOUTHCOATES STATION HOTEL, HOLDERNESS ROAD
97. SHEPHERD INN, WITHAM
98. HOLDERNESS NEW INN, WITHAM
99. BLUE BELL HOTEL, WITHAM
100. NOAH'S ARK INN, WITHAM
101. HOPE & ANCHOR INN, CLEVELAND STREET
102. GRAPES TAVERN, LIME STREET
103. SHIP LAUNCH INN, LIME STREET
104. SHOULDER OF MUTTON, LIME STREET
105. SHIP INN, STONEFERRY *not shown on map

85. NORTH BRIDGE INN, WITHAM

An inn of some sort had stood on this site since the end of the 18th century. In 1817 Thomas Marshall, victualler and rope maker, was recorded at North Bridge Foot and was one of the first recorded victuallers of the North Bridge Inn.

Many addresses have been applied to the inn including Witham, Garrison Side, Bridge Foot and North Bridge Street. The opening of the new North Bridge in 1931 left the inn somewhat isolated and in 1941 it fell victim to the bombing raids that narrowly missed the new bridge itself.

The official date of closure was 9th May 1941 and the licence was later transferred to the new Mermaid, Bethune Avenue, in 1959.

86. CARPENTERS ARMS, GREAT UNION STREET

The Carpenters Arms was first mentioned in 1806 when Thomas England (the Constable of Sutton and a Cordwainer by trade) was the first victualler. It was one of the first taverns to be built in Great Union Street, which was laid out in 1803, and stood on the east side of the street between Coeleus Street and Hyperion Street.

The Carpenters' was also known as the Shipwright's Arms during the 1820s and 1830s. Both names were reflections of the local trades and Friendly Societies would have met there at one time or another. The Carpenters' closed following redundancy in March 1937 and was heavily bombed in 1941. The site is now a second-hand car lot.

87. COMMERCIAL HOTEL, GREAT UNION STREET

The site of the Commercial Hotel is now a set of traffic lights at the junction of Clarence Street and Great Union Street.

The hotel was first opened as a 'coffee house', which was no more than an attractive name for an alehouse. It was built around 1800 and enjoyed excellent trade from the nearby timber and shipbuilding yards as well as visitors to the Drypool Cattle Markets.

Sadly, its position was to be its downfall as in 1941 German bombers, following the line of the river Hull, caused extensive damage to the nearby Ranks Mills and the Commercial was in the line of fire. Severely damaged, the remains were finally cleared in 1952.

88. ORDNANCE ARMS, GREAT UNION STREET

The Ordnance Arms opened circa 1810. Originally a much smaller property than the one shown, it was bought by brewer William Glossop in the late 19th century and enlarged to take in the shop next door.

In the impressive new frontage Glossop included his initials and the date of rebuilding, which was probably 1884 but is partly obscured in this photograph. Following the extension of Clarence Street to join Holderness Road in 1889 the Ordnance was one of a trio of inns at the busiest junction in Drypool and enjoyed excellent trade.

The Ordnance Arms suffered an almost direct hit in May 1941 during one of Hull's worst nights of bombing and the remains were demolished soon after.

89. WATERLOO TAVERN, HARCOURT STREET

The 'Bush' at the corner of Great Union Street and Clarence Street is a popular stopping-off point for drinkers on Friday night tours of Hull's Old Town pubs. It would surprise many of them to know that the original Waterloo Tavern could be traced back to the days of Napoleon and possibly earlier.

Wellington's victory at Waterloo in 1815 was certainly the inspiration for the naming (or re-naming) of the building shown in this photograph. Purchased by the Hull Brewery Co. in 1919, it was rebuilt in 1932.

After suffering slight damage in the Second World War it was repaired in the 1950s. Its original address, Harcourt Street, can still be seen as a street sign on the front of the building.

90. RAILWAY INN, HEDON ROAD

This beer-house stood on the south side of Hedon Road just west of the junction with Popple Street. The building was shown on the 1853 Ordnance Survey Plan as part of 'Marine Terrace' but no record of it appeared in the trade directories until 1857.

George Thompson, victualler at the Blue Bell in nearby Thomas Street, opened the inn which took its name from the nearby Victoria Railway terminus less than a hundred yards to the east.

It closed in December 1933 and the licence was transferred to the new Endyke Hotel, Endike Lane. Yet another victim of German bombers during the war the building, which was by then a café, was demolished in the 1940s.

A plain breeze-block wall now marks the site.

91. DOVER CASTLE HOTEL, HEDON ROAD

Ralph Smith opened a beer-house at the corner of Merrick Street and Hedon Road circa 1870. In 1877 a full licence was obtained from the redundant Regatta Tavern in High Street and the name Dover Castle was given to the premises.

The pub was large by local standards and had ornate brown-glazed tiles around the whole of its frontage. Internally, the serving counters of each room were decorated with multicoloured ceramic tiles.

The Dover Castle ceased trading in the 1950s but the buildings were kept in use by various businesses in the following years. The building survives to this day but any clues to its history are long gone.

92. ALBION HOTEL, HEDON ROAD

The Albion Hotel stood at the corner of Hedon Road and Williamson Street in one form or another from at least 1867 when it was first recorded in the trade directories.

It enjoyed good trade, being opposite the North Eastern Railway's Victoria Goods Station at a time when Hedon Road was bustling with transport of every kind travelling to and from the busy Victoria and Alexandra Docks.

The building was badly damaged and subsequently demolished following bombing in 1941. The licence was held in suspension until 1960 and then transferred to the new Crooked Billet, Holderness Road.

93. ORIENTAL HOTEL, HEDON ROAD

The derelict buildings of the now closed Oriental Hotel currently await demolition on the south side of Hedon Road near to the entrance of the Alexandra Dock. The bland 1950's architecture of this derelict Oriental (opened 6th February 1958) gives no clue to the nature of the building that it replaced.

The original Oriental Hotel shown in this photograph of 1910 stood on the opposite side of the road at the corner of Woodhouse Street. 'Oriental' was probably a reference to the varied nationalities of its customers, many of whom would have been foreign seamen fresh from ship.

The pub continued to enjoy excellent trade until the Second World War when German bombers scored an accidental hit whilst attempting to bomb the docks on 8th May 1941, resulting in its immediate closure.

94. BLUE BELL INN, THOMAS STREET

A gardener John Johnson had large Strawberry Gardens in this part of Drypool at the beginning of the 19th century. Around 1815 he built the first Blue Bell on this site, originally known as Green Lane but more familiar now as Thomas Street. The Blue Bell stood on the west side of the street opposite the entrance to Merrick Street.

In 1894, following its purchase by Bass Ratcliffe & Gretton, it was rebuilt with an attractive ceramic tiled frontage and the obligatory huge gas lamp hanging over the door. Competition was strong in the area and lack of trade due to wide-scale slum clearance hastened the demise of the Blue Bell and in 1938 it closed having been declared redundant.

95. SHIPWRIGHT'S ARMS, MARVEL STREET

This corner site was originally developed as two shops, one of which later became a beer-house. Curved brickwork like this was a common feature of many corner pubs in the days of the Shipwright's Arms.

Following its purchase by the Hull Brewery Co. in 1891 it was enlarged and re-fronted. Although still a small beer-house it had been enlarged slightly to make two rooms - a smoke room (or snug) and a larger bar, both having doors to separate streets.

Having survived the ravages of slum clearance in the 1930s, the Shipwright's Arms suffered bomb damage during the war and was demolished in the late 1940s.

96. SOUTHCOATES STATION HOTEL, HOLDERNESS ROAD

Opposite the Corn Mill Hotel on the north side of Holderness Road is a street that now appears to have no name. It was originally Beeton Street, laid out in the early 1850s though not built upon until the 1860s.

In a trade directory of 1872 R.Bubbins was recorded as victualler at the Railway Arms, situated at the corner of Beeton Street. William Glossop & Bulay Ltd. purchased and enlarged the premises at the end of the 19th century. Soon after it became the Southcoates Station Hotel, named after the nearby station on the Hull to Withernsea line.

The Hotel suffered bomb damage and was closed in 1941. The licence was held in suspension until 1961 when it was transferred to the new Pelican Hotel, James Reckitt Avenue.

97. SHEPHERD INN, WITHAM

Originally named the Bull & Dog, the Shepherd was built circa 1780, its name being a reference to the 'sport' of bull baiting. As was frequently the case a new landlord brought a new name and the Bull & Dog became the Shepherd Inn during the 1830s. This may be a reference to the formation of the Royal Order of Ancient Shepherds, Hull District, in 1839.

When Samuel G. Doyle took over circa 1880 the Shepherd became known as the Audacious. He had been an officer on HM Ship Audacious and his name can be seen on the name board over the inn.

The minutes of the Hull Sanitary Commission confirm the Shepherd was demolished along with Holderness Court in the winter of 1901. The arched entrance to Holderness Court can just be seen to the left of this photograph and survives to the present day.

98. HOLDERNESS NEW INN, WITHAM

This rather plain public house was first known as the Holderness Tavern and built circa 1800. By 1826 it had become the Holderness New Inn.

Some confusion arose when another tavern opened at the junction of Witham and Dansom Lane in 1840 with the same name. The second tavern was soon re-named the Holderness Hotel.

Possibly the first recorded licensee of the Holderness New Inn was a Richard Smithson in 1806 and at that time it would have appeared as a very simple house with little decoration.

Following its purchase by Gleadow & Dibb (later the Hull Brewery Co.) in 1870 it was rebuilt circa 1880. It closed in the 1970s but the building remains almost intact and is currently up for sale.

99. BLUE BELL HOTEL, WITHAM

The Blue Bell started life as a small building with stables circa 1780. Its name was probably taken from the name of a common local flower - the harebell - although the sign that hung outside would probably have been of a blue bell. It remained open as the Blue Bell throughout the 19th century. It had been a very popular meeting place for local horse racing enthusiasts and the St.Leger cup was exhibited on the premises in 1825 following a win by the horse 'Lottery'.

After the widening of Witham circa 1900 the building line was set back and the property re-built to three storeys. After the First World War trade suffered and the pub closed. The licence of the Blue Bell was transferred to the new Five Ways, Boothferry Road circa 1932.

The building survives near the Cleveland Street junction and is now the premises of a household appliance spares shop.

100. NOAH'S ARK INN, WITHAM

This pub was possibly named after one of its first victuallers, Noah Robinson, a blacksmith of Witham around 1800. It was built circa 1770 and changed its name to the Wellington around 1812 but reverted to the name Noah's Ark due to the fall in popularity of the Duke of Wellington after he became Prime Minister.

A road linking Witham and the old Cleveland Street to the north had been suggested as early as the 1860s and the council purchased many properties in this area at the turn of the century in preparation for the construction of the new road.

The Noah's Ark Inn was closed in 1903 and the property was then used as a dwelling house. It was reported as "standing empty and awaiting demolition" in the 1904-05 Hull Sanitary Committee minutes. The Corporation took this photograph of the derelict property prior to demolition in 1905.

101. HOPE & ANCHOR INN, CLEVELAND STREET

Following the construction of Cleveland Street in the early 19th century some of the first buildings to have been built along the route were likely to have been inns and taverns.

The Hope & Anchor, a small alehouse, was recorded around 1840. The sign of the Hope & Anchor was common in areas with a strong shipping link and usually pictured a comforting female figure clasping an anchor.

The original building was completely rebuilt in 1938 and turned into a club in the 1970s. The site is currently within the Spiders nightclub.

102. GRAPES TAVERN, LIME STREET

The Grapes Inn stood at the corner of Lime Street and Jenning Street and opened soon after Jenning Street was laid out around 1800. Consequently its first address was Jenning Street.

It was first known locally as the Barrack Tavern as much of its early custom would have come from the soldiers based in the Hull Garrison further north in Lime Street, and for a short time in warehouses next to the inn. Although known as the Barrack Tavern, it would have had the most common sign for a public house, a bunch of grapes, hanging outside. Following the closure of the Garrison it became known simply as the Grapes Tavern.

The pub closed around 1960 but fragments of the building remain.

103. SHIP LAUNCH INN, LIME STREET

The first recorded victualler of this alehouse was Mathew Heslewood, who was recorded as a victualler in 'Limas Street' in 1791. In 1803 he was listed in a trade directory at the Sawyers' Arms, Lime Street.

Most of the drinking establishments in this area reflected local trades in their name and much of the land opposite the Sawyers Arms was taken up with timber yards and dry docks. By 1826 its name had changed to the Ship Launch, another trade reference.

Following the 1904 Licensing Act three Lime Street pubs were closed including the Ship Launch, for which the owners received £2050 compensation. It was later demolished as part of a slum clearance scheme.

104. SHOULDER OF MUTTON, LIME STREET

No buildings were shown on the site of the Shoulder of Mutton on either the 1835 or 1842 plans of Hull. By the time of the first Ordnance Survey plan in 1853 the buildings of Brooke & Tate's Groves Brewery are shown on what was probably the site of former barracks.

The Shoulder of Mutton was recorded in the trade directories from 1855 when it was the 'tap' for the brewery. The buildings were part of a purchase agreement when the Hull Brewery Co. took over Tate's in 1896. At this point the pub was rebuilt as it appears in this photograph of circa 1925.

The Shoulder of Mutton suffered badly when the vast numbers of houses in the 'Groves' district were gradually demolished in the slum clearance schemes before and after the Second World War and it was closed on the 5th February 1959.

105. SHIP INN, STONEFERRY

A bit 'off the beaten track' but worthy of inclusion is this original version of the Ship Inn, first recorded as the Sloop in the 1820s.

It is very likely that the building in this photograph was the same one that had stood on this site, on the edge of the riverbank, since the end of the 18th century and probably much earlier. At the foot of the building the brickwork is obviously of a very early date.

The plan of the building also shows its layout to be of a very early style and suggestive of what is known as a "middle level long house with baffle entrance", common in the mid to late 17th century.

The building was demolished in 1932 when the present Ship was built further east fronting Ann Watson Street.

BIBLIOGRAPHY

A History of English Ale & Beer. H.A.Monckton. Bodley Head, London, 1966.

A History of Hull. E. Gillett & K.A. MacMahon.1980, revised reprinted edition. Hull University Press, 1989.

A New Picture of Georgian Hull. Ivan and Elizabeth Hall. William Sessions Ltd., York and Hull Civic Society, 1978/79.

Barley Mash & Yeast: A History of the Hull Brewery Company 1782-1985. Robert Barnard. Hutton Press Ltd., and Hull College, 1990.

British Inn Signs and their stories. Eric R.Delderfield. David & Charles, Newton Abbott, 1965.

Desirable Abodes for all Parties Visiting Hull. (Some of the Hotels, Inns, Taverns and Beer Houses in the Waterworks Street area) Unpublished notes. Paul L. Gibson. Hull, 1997.

History of the Streets of Hull. W. Sykes (from J. Richardson's manuscripts-originally published in the Hull & E. Yorkshire Times, 1915). Malet Lambert reprint, Hull, 1980.

Hull and East Yorkshire Breweries. Pat Aldabella and Robert Barnard. East Yorkshire Local History Society, 1997.

Hull In The 1950's: A Pictorial Diary of Life in Kingston upon Hull. John E. Smith. Hutton Press Ltd., Cherry Burton, 1994.

Inns of Holderness and Taverns of East Hull. John Wilson Smith (Edited by Robert Barnard). Local History Unit, Hull College, 1996.

"It was a lovely shopping street!" 190 years of the development, history, shops and people of Charles Street. Mike Ayres. Unpublished notes. Local History Unit, Hull College, 1994.

Landlord. Unpublished notes on Hull's pubs. Graham Wilkinson, 1998.

Last Orders Please! Index Edition. (A Guide to the Lost Hotels, Inns, Taverns and Beer-Houses that Once Served Hull's Old Town). Richard Hayton. Hull College, Local History Unit, 1996.

Living and Dying in Hull: A Picture of Hull in the Nineteenth century. Bernard Foster. Privately published, Hull, 1984.

Lost Churches and Chapels of Hull. David Neave, with Geoff Bell, Christopher Ketchell and Susan Neave. Hull City Museums & Art Galleries and the Hutton Press, 1991.

Moors' & Robson's Breweries Ltd. A Brief History. Robert Barnard. Local History Unit, Hull College, 1996.

Notes Relative to the Manor of Myton. J. Travis Cook. Hull, 1890.

Paragonia-The Paragon Street Story. P.L.Gibson. Unpublished notes. Hull, 1998.

PUBS *Understanding listing.* English Heritage. London, 1994.

Rough notes on Wincolmlee Pubs. Robert Barnard. Local History Unit, Hull College. 1998.

The Beverley Road Walk ("a noble approach to the town"). Christopher Ketchell. Unpublished notes. Local History Unit, Hull College, 1997.

The Buildings of England. Yorkshire: York and the East Riding. Nikolaus Pevsner and David Neave. Penguin Books, Second Edition, 1995.

The Old Friendly Societies of Hull. Paul Davis. A.Brown & Sons Ltd., Hull, 1926.

The Oxford Illustrated History of Britain. Kenneth O. Morgan. Guild Publishing Ltd., London, 1984.

"Tremendous Activity in the Old Town", List of buildings demolished in Hull 1943-1988. C.J.Ketchell. Local History Unit, Hull College, Revised Edition, 1989.

Victoria County History of the County of York and the East Riding. Volume 1. The City of Kingston upon Hull. Edited by K.J. Allison. Oxford University Press for Institute of Historical Research, 1969.

INDEX   entries in bold indicate photographs

Also from Kingston Press

TOWN and GUN

Audrey Howes and Martin Foreman

Focusing on a period when Hull was at the centre of national events, from Civil War to Glorious Revolution, *Town and Gun* tells the 'secret history' of the city's 17th century defences through contemporary documents and archaeological evidence. *Town and Gun* explores not only the massive remains of the Hull Citadel but also the lives and work of their builders, the soldiers and the families who lived and died alongside them.

Town and Gun price £9.95

ISBN 1 902039 02 5

FORGOTTEN HULL

Graham Wilkinson and Gareth Watkins

Hull's social history is brought to life in this fascinating pictorial record of the city, showing what it was like to live in Hull between the 1890s and 1930s.
Forgotten Hull is a magnificent collection of over 100 meticulously researched historical photographs of the city and surrounding area, faithfully restored and reproduced from the original glass plate negatives and mounted prints of the Hull Corporation Health Department.

Forgotten Hull price £12.75

ISBN 1 902039 00 9

DAN BILLANY

Valerie A. Reeves and Valerie Showan

Born in 1913 into a poor Hull family, Dan Billany fought tenaciously to achieve his ambitions - a university degree, a job as a teacher and eventually fame as a best-selling author in Britain and the USA.
Dan Billany - Hull's lost hero, is a carefully researched biography contrasting his adventures as a soldier, a prisoner of war and as a fugitive on the run in Italy with the inner turmoil of a man coming to terms with his homosexuality - a life cruelly cut short and enormous potential unrealised.

Dan Billany price £6.25

ISBN 1 902039 01 7

Orders and Enquiries

Kingston Press,
Hull Central Library,
Albion Street
Kingston upon Hull
United Kingdom
HU1 3TF

Telephone: (01482) 616814
Fax: (01482) 616827
E-Mail: kpress@hullcc.demon.co.uk